Alexander Täuschel

Linguistic Aspects in Machine Translation

Alexander Täuschel

Linguistic Aspects in Machine Translation

GRIN Verlag

Bibliografische Information der Deutschen Nationalbibliothek: Die Deutsche Bibliothek verzeichnet diese Publikation in der Deutschen Nationalbibliografie; detaillierte bibliografische Daten sind im Internet über http://dnb.d-nb.de/ abrufbar.

1. Auflage 2006
Copyright © 2006 GRIN Verlag
http://www.grin.com/
Druck und Bindung: Books on Demand GmbH, Norderstedt Germany
ISBN 978-3-640-19614-2

2006

Linguistic Aspects in Machine Translation

This paper will give a general overview of the venture that is machine translation with particular focus on linguistic aspects. It will display history of MT and will deal with some of the major issues in the realisation of MT like the difficulty of translating prepositions or integrating semantics, as well as the importance of real world knowledge. To illustrate these difficulties with examples on a basic level, a practice test with a moderately complex translation engine provided by Google has been carried out and will be explained. Finally, I am going to introduce three of the largest and most powerful translation machines currently in use. I will also give a brief over-view of methods of MT. The aim of this paper is to show that the realisation of the primal idea of machine translation in its original sense, which was to perform translation without human intervention (except during the construction phase of the system), is still markedly far away at present and machines are still unlikely to take over the jobs of human translators.

Alexander Täuschel
18.01.2006

Table of Contents

I.   Introduction

I. 1.)   What is Machine Translation?

A translation machine is a specialised software system developed for the translating from one human language to another: "[Machine translation systems are actually not *machines*, rather to be thought of] as programs that run on computers, which really are machines" (Arnold et al. 1994:10). Machine translation, or as it was called in its early days: Mechanical Translation (henceforth abbreviated as MT) is a subfield of artificial intelligence (AI), both belonging to the large area of computer science (CS).

The field of machine translation is widely considered as one of the most awkward issues in computational linguistics, because it requires interdisciplinary knowledge of the scientists involved in the development of translation machines: knowledge in informatics, language cognition, skills in translating and in language description methods, as well as specialised knowledge in the fields the texts, which are to be translated, deal with (see: Schwanke 1991:11).

Furthermore, if translation machines were able to take over translational work completely, they would have to cover all capacities of a human translator: Human translators have to set a pragmatical or aesthetical balance between the source text and the target text (see: Wilss 1988:VII). Applying skills, as well as language and transcultural knowledge are some of the translator's optional tools to reach the expectations of the source text writer and the target text reader. Another tool, according to Wilss, was a translator's "intuition". He suggests that it was "some kind of sixth sense", "the opposite of calculatable dynamics", a part of the translator's mysterious, notorious "black box", whose existence was not unknown, but which we only had an *intuitive* image of. Wilss adds that intuition was a "mental axiom" that could not be challenged (129).

So if a translator's 'intuition' is so hard to define, how can it be synthesised within computer software, within a machine?

For a start, these reasons can only give a clue of what is at least involved in the development of translation machines. Thus, the enthusiasm and belief in the future of computers taking over and handling the translation of human languages has see-sawed since the birthing of its idea.

I. 2.)   Why Machine Translation Matters

MT was "one of the earliest applications" (Arnold et al. 1994:iii) suggested for digital[1] computers[2] and like an artist might argue that a painting is never really finished, the whole development of computer science is still in process – and so is the "long-term scientific dream" of MT.

Also, the issue of MT contains increasing importance in several different fields of human enterprise; which will be explained in the following:

I. 2. a)   Social and Political Importance of MT

Its social and political importance "arises from the socio-political importance of translation in communities where more than one language is generally spoken" (4), and where the adoption of a common lingua franca is proximate. This – on the other hand – involves the dominance of the chosen language among the community to the disadvantage of the speakers of the other language(s).

---

[1] *digit* (lat.): finger (Savetz)
[2] *computare* (lat.): to reckon (Savetz)

This other language(s) can then become "second class" or disappear in the worst case, which is undoubtedly something that should matter, because it involves potential loss of culture as well as ways and uses of thinking and living. "So translation is necessary for communication (…)", even if it means putting up with the side effects of it, like modifying or by chance, even losing semantic or/and cultural details of the information which is to be translated into a different language, and to be made accessible for another cultural community respectively. But since the modern world's demand for translation "far outstrips any possible supply", that is because of the actual deficiency of human translators and capacity; "the automation of translation is a social and political necessity for modern societies which do not wish to impose a common language on their members". Cases like the Spanish speaking parts of the USA or the Welsh speaking parts of Great Britain make this point obvious. Switzerland or the European Community, in which multilingualism is part of every-day life, even more do so.

I. 2. b)   Scientific Importance of MT

The scientific importance of MT results from its quality of being an interesting application and testing ground for ideas in CS, AI, and Linguistics – from which some of the most important developments have begun in MT, like: the origins of Prolog,[3] the first widely available logic programming language, which formed a key part of the Japanese Fifth Generation programme,[4] were originally developed for MT (see: 5).

I. 2. c)   Commercial Importance of MT

In today's world of business the commercial importance of MT is not to be underestimated. Firstly: As a matter of accessibility, a customer is more probable to buy a Japanese product with a manual written in English than one whose manual is written in Japanese; even more so, when having to buy a safety critical system. Secondly: translation is expensive and requires highly skilled (and paid) workers. An average human translator may be able to manage 4-6 pages a day (see: 1994:5), which may cause delays during the development and the launching of a new product. Up to 40-45% of the running costs of European Community institutions are 'language costs', "of which translating and interpreting are the main element" (1994:5). The costs per year would make out about £300 million – a figure only relating to translations actually being done, not the amount of translation being required (see: Patterson 1982).

I. 2. d)   Philosophical Importance of MT

MT is also a philosophical challenge, because "it represents the attempt to automate an activity that can require the full range of human knowledge (…): "The extend to which one can automate translation is an indication of the extend to which one can automate 'thinking'" (Arnold et al. 1994:5).

---

[3] *Prolog* = short for PROgramming in LOGic was created by Alain Colmerauer (1941-) et al. in Marseille during the 1970s. At the University of Edinburgh the work was finished with the support of Clocksin and Mellish. And today their version called Edinburgh syntax is commonly acknowledged as standard (see: <www.pcai.com>.)
[4] *Fifth Generation* = a "Japanese billion-dollar project, with a target date of 1989 to design and build a computer that is not only a hundred times faster than a Cray 'supercomputer' (the so-called Cray-1 system which was built by Cray Inc. in 1976 with a speed of 160 megaflops and an 8 MB memory; for further information see: www.cray.com) but contains AI software as well" (Savetz); also see chapter III. 3.) of this paper.

II.   The History of Machine Translation

II. 1.)   The First Years of Translation Machines

Ideas about mechanising translation processes can be traced back to the seventeenth century, in connection with ideas on 'real characters' and 'universal' or 'philosophical languages', but it was not until the 20th century, until it came to realistic possibilities: In the mid 1930s, a French-Armenian, named Georges Artsrouni and a Russian, named Petr Smirnov-Trojanskij, who remained unrecognized in the USSR (See: Schwanke 1991:69), both applied for patents for 'translating machines'. Their idea contained not only a method for an automatic bilingual dictionary, but also a scheme for coding interlingual grammatical roles, based on Esperanto, and ideas for analysing sentences and generating texts in other languages. Neither one of them nor their ideas were known to anyone involved in the latter putting forward of the first tentative ideas for using the new invention – computers – for translating natural languages.

Pioneers in MT came from a wide variety of backgrounds, like electrical engineering, physics, linguistics, interpretation or philosophy. Two of these pioneers were Andrew Booth and Warren Weaver (1894-1978), who are particularly referred to in chapter II. 2.) of this paper.

In the earliest period, the question of what constituted an intermediary language ('interlingua';[5] which is how the actual part of work done by the translation machine is named, because the whole act required – and still requires – pre-editing and post-editing by a human; see: Schwanke 1991:69) and how it might be created preoccupied many researchers. It was closely related to in the minds of many at the time with what was seen as parallel activity in the field of information retrieval[6] towards a universally applicable 'information language'. The public interest and the attention of those different scientific disciplines drawn to this new task was widespread to such extend, that it was not surprising that presentations of MT took place at a wide range of conferences, wherever there was interest in the use of computers for exploring language and communication; for instance conferences on cybernetics, information retrieval, linguistics etc. The publicity which statements about the immediate prospects of working systems attracted was not always welcome by those in the field, because it raised the public hopes higher and higher.

With time, the attention was drawn to the limitations of dictionary-based systems and to the importance of analysing and transforming syntactic structures; and from the 1960s onwards the common focus of nearly all the MT groups was on syntax. There was initial interest in the theories of Chomsky, but in time computers for syntactic structure analysis developed independently of the dominant developments in theoretical linguistics. The basic system design moved away from the earlier 'direct translation' approach[7], and overall design was tending towards a three (or more) stage approach involving independent processes of analysis, transfer, and synthesis.

Pioneers in MT had to face manifold and complex problems:

- Computers were for a long time limited in storage and speed, expensive to use and not widely available (in the case of the USSR unavailable until the 1970s, and even then they were far behind American models in capacity and speed).
- Input was cumbersome: texts had to be laboriously coded onto punched cards, because most groups devised their own coding systems.

---

[5] also see V. 1.) of this paper
[6] *information retrieval* = the use of computers to indentify and access documents relevant to particular query (see: Hutchins 2000:2)
[7] *direct translation* = essentially built on word-for-word lexical substitution and structure modification (see: 3)

- A recurrent demand at the time was for optical character readers, which was not realised until the 1980s.
- The output was in the form reams of large sheets of computer paper, often nearly illegible.
- Off-line storage was either on punched cards or on paper or on steel magnetized tapes.

The pre-occupation of researchers' minds through the problems of dictionary storage and accurate access led to the development of procedures which are taken for granted nowadays.

II. 2.)   A Pioneer: Warren Weaver, Founder of the Idea of MT

Warren Weaver was born on the 17th July 1894 in Reedsburg, Wisconsin, of German descent. Interested in engineering and gifted with talent his career took him from graduating in civil engineering over teaching mathematics at the Throop College in Pasadena, California, to being appointed director of the Natural Science Division of the Rockefeller Foundation, where he inaugurated programs to support quantitative experimental biology and molecular biology. During the war he directed the work of several hundred mathematicians on operations research at the Office of Scientific Research and Development, to which he was invited by Vannevar Bush (1890-1974).[8] Weaver carried out a globally important program of agricultural research in Central and South America, India and the Philippines. He collaborated with Richard Courant[9] in plans for strengthening advanced mathematics research in the United States, and the establishment of the Courant Institute of New York University, whose main building is called 'Warren Weaver Hall'. He also wrote many articles in popular science, "Comments on the general theory of air warfare" among them, which was a significant factor in the founding of the 'RAND Corporation'.[10] Weaver was very fond of Carrol's *Alice's Adventures in Wonderland* (1962) and has built up a collection of translations of it.

The first time Weaver had mentioned the possibility of using the computer to translate was in March 1947, when he wrote a letter to the cyberneticist Norbert Wiener, who was not interested in this idea, but soon after that[11] Weaver talked about it with Andrew Booth,[12] a British x-ray crystallographer, who was working on ideas for a mechanical dictionary. By 1949, Weaver was urged by colleagues at the Rockefeller Foundation to elaborate his ideas in a memorandum, which he was supposed to send to 20 or 30 acquaintances:

"I have a text in front of me which is written in Russian, but I am going to pretend that it is really written in English and that it has been coded in some strange symbols. All I need to do is strip off the code in order to retrieve the information contained in the text."
(Warren Weaver, as cited in Arnold et al. 1994:13).

---

[8] *Bush, Vannevar* (1890-1974): pivotal figure in hypertext research; concepted MEMEX (a device in which an individual stores all his books, records, and communications), which was the first idea of an "easily accessible, individually configurable storehouse of knowledge" (Keep et al. (2001).
[9] *Courant, Richard* (1888-1972): German mathematician, founder of the *Courant Institute for Mathematical Sciences* (since 1964) at New York University (see: <www-history.mcs.st-and.ac.uk>)
[10] *The RAND Corporation* about themselves on their website: "The RAND Corporation is a non-profit research organization providing objective analysis and effective solutions that address the challenges facing the public and private sectors around the world". Its name derived from a contraction of the term *research and development*. They have dealt with packet switching (seed of the internet) in 1962, water resource management in Netherlands in 1976, and the expanding of the NATO in 1995 (Lewis 2004).
[11] Schwanke states that this conversation had in fact already taken place in the year 1946 (1991:69).
[12] also see chapter II. 1.) of this paper

This sentence, taken out of that memorandum, traces the actual development of MT, since it is not quite clear, who was in fact the first one that had the idea of translating automatically between human languages. This memorandum "sparked a significant amount of interest and research" (13), "written before most people had any idea of what computers might be capable of, it was the direct stimulus for the beginnings of research in the US" (Hutchins 2000:17). According to Schwanke, this was assumably so, because the works of Booth and his colleagues had not been well-known in the U.S. at that time (see: 1991:70).

Weaver believed in the code system, which Booth had especially developed for Weaver's idea and he was also convinced, that difficulties of semantic ambiguity could be solved particularly in technical languages by adding a sufficient context. Schwanke states, that the enthusiasm, with which Weaver's memorandum was being commonly complemented as a milestone in the history of MT, was retrospectively irreproducible.

Later, by the 1950s, a large number of groups researched on the idea in Europe and the USA, not to mention the financial investment of about £20,000,000 (Arnold et al. 1994:13). Unfortunately it was not met with much success, and doubts arose about the possibility of automating translation (at least in the current state of knowledge). According to Arnold et al., the philosopher Bar-Hillel[13] announced especially FAHQMT, as principally impossible in a 1959 report. But this did not mean that MT in general was impossible.

Weaver displayed the main issues he saw for changing MT for the better in his memorandum of 1949 as the "Three Levels of Problems in Communication" (Gibbon 1998):

Level A: How accurately can the symbols of communication be transmitted?
(The technical problem)

Level B: How precisely do the transmitted symbols convey the desired meaning? (The semantic problem)

Level C: How effectively does the received meaning affect conduct in the desired way? (The problem of effectiveness)

According to Gibbon (1998), there was close relation between those three levels and the so-called semiotic distinctions:

A: Syntax and the forms of language
B: Semantics and the meanings of language
C: Pragmatics and the use or function of language.

Warren Weaver's memorandum lead to the convening of the first MT conference in the Princeton Inn, in July 1960 and the first book-length treatment, with a foreword written by Weaver. In this, he states his optimism for MT:

"[It is] not to charm or delight, not to contribute to elegance or beauty; but to be of wide service in the work-a-day task of making available the essential content of documents in languages which are foreign to the reader." (Hutchins 2000:20).

According to Hutchins, Warren Weaver's words have proved.

---

[13] *Bar-Hillel, Yehoshua* (1915-1975): philosopher, who had been a central figure in the early development of the field and contributed what should be considered "the first set of sober assessments for MT", believed that, "in order to achieve Fully Automatic High-Quality Machine Translation (FAHQMT), machines must be able to process meaning" (Nirenburg 2003).

II. 3.)   The Latter Years in MT

According to Hutchins, the best-known event in the history of MT was the publication of the ALPAC report by the 'Automatic Language Processing Advisory Committee' in November 1966. It was established for the Pentagon, and made MT appear as generally unrealisable to the public. The report suggested for instance, that it might in fact be "simpler and more economical for heavy users of Russian translations to learn to read the documents in the original language" (see: <http://webcenters.netscape.compuserve.com>). The report disrupted almost any research in MT worldwide, "in ignorance of the successful, cost-effective applications already in place" (Slocum 1988:25). "For years afterwards, an interest in MT was something to keep quiet about; it was almost shameful" (see: http://webcenters.netscape.compuserve.com>) – until the 1980s, when firms like Siemens AG took on the METAL project[14] and the Japanese government launched the Fifth-Generation,[15] which was based on the programming language Prolog.

The fact that universities, governments and factories teamed up with each other worldwide lead to the first translation machines for personal computers as only one result and made Japan the world's leader of MT research today.

There are only up to 20 active companies in today's MT software world market, due to the so-called dotcom[16] crash during 2000-2001, when during a phase of common internet euphoria many little start ups, so-called dotcom-companies, were founded and some of them grew rich and huge in such a short amount of time, that all the others could not remain on the market and simply disappeared again, while only the big ones stood the test.

Many products in the world market of MT are licensed, so the false impression of a larger number of companies to choose from is created. In fact, the research and developing of translation machines mainly takes place at universities today.

III.   Machine Translation in Practice

To illustrate a view of MT from a PC user's level, this chapter will take a look at dealing with the restrictiveness of MT when it is used as an internet tool (= engine), for instance, since nowadays the internet is accessible to many individuals, at least it is in Western countries; but the number of people having the ability increases hourly. Anybody who can take access to the internet can use translation engines in his everyday life or professionally, although Arnold et al. state that "the use of MT (...) is completely unknown to the vast majority of individuals and organizations in the world, even those involved in the so-called 'language industries', like translators, terminologists, technical writers, etc. (1994:19). Assumingly, during the development of Arnold's book it still was, since that book was written in 1994. But according to the European Association for Machine Translation,[17] "the internet has proven to be a huge stimulus for MT", so I consider translation machines appearing as internet tools being relevant.

---

[14] also see: V. 2. b) of this work
[15] also see: I. 1. b) of this paper
[16] *dotcom* = stock-market for internet and telecommunication shares
[17] The *European Association for Machine Translation* in their own words: "The European Association for Machine Translation (EAMT) is an organization that serves the growing community of people interested in MT and translation tools, including users, developers and researchers of this increasingly viable technology." (for further information see: <http://www.eamt.org >)

III. 1.)   MT Test: Google

The internet offers several options to operate with natural languages, like Google[18] for instance. Primarily, Google[19] is a search engine, which is a machine supposed to find websites with particular contents, phrases, words or pictures on demand, but besides that it also offers many more services, like a translation engine: One may require to translate websites en bloc, or choose to use a subsite of Google on which he may pick from several "language pairs" (Schwanke 1991:218), like 'from English to Korean' or 'from Spain to English', then insert a word, sentence or text in the input field, then get a result in the chosen target language from the output field.

By trying out this translation software one can easily come across some of the drawbacks and restrictiveness of MT. It will not make any sense to choose any text, put it through the engine and use the output right away. One will have to take the machine's restrictiveness into account, consider "pre-editing" and "post-editing" (Arnold et al. 1994:12). The first restriction is the genre of the text that is to be translated by the engine. I would like to demonstrate this with an example.

Example 1:   From German to English

INPUT:

(a made up sentence)
Es war einmal ein verflixter Wurm, der kroch quer über das ganze Land.

OUTPUT:

It was once a verflixter worm, crept crosswise over the whole country.

The sentence in the target language English may nearly match the sense of the sentence in the source language German. But the first thing that meets the eye is the word 'verflixter': Obviously the software was not able to associate this word with any expression from the Geman lexical store, so it was left untranslated. Another mistake would be to translate 'es war einmal' into 'it was once'. If at all, it should say 'there was once'; but of course the appropriate British English equivalent would be 'once upon a time'. The engine also seems to have ignored the reflexive pronoun 'der', which should have been translated to 'that' or 'which', the usual reflexive pronouns used in the English language. Furthermore 'crosswise' would not quite say the same as 'quer', which was more likely to be in accordance with 'across'. In the original sense of the example sentence, putting the verb 'criss-crossed' instead of 'crept crosswise', along with leaving out any translation of the adverb 'quer', might also do.

Example 2:   From English to German

INPUT:

(a made up sentence)
So I picked up the phone and dialed your number.

OUTPUT:

So hob ich das Telefon auf und wählte Ihre Nummer.

---

[18] Officially internet language tools are considered "cheap" and not representative for complex developed translation machines like METEO or LOGOS which will also be dealt with in this paper).
[19] Google's website is currently available in 104 natural languages; Swahili, Zulu and Scottish-Gaelic among them.

This example demonstrates two major effects:

One is the mistranlation of idioms, like 'I picked up the phone', which would be correctly translated in its original sense with a) 'ich nahm das Telefon ab' or b) 'ich nahm das Telefon in die Hand' or c) 'ich nahm mir das Telefon'. All of these options seem right at hand for a human mind, familiar with the English and German language, but not necessarily for the abilities of a translation engine (or a translation machine).

Effect number two is the disability of applying the T/V distinction.[20] Representing formal distance to the addressee by using 'Sie' instead of 'du' (or 'vous'/'Usted' instead of 'tu'/'tu') might be appropriate when speaking (or writing) to a person of higher social status or a person that is not familiar. But it might also express irony or a distance where not appropriate, within family relations, for instance. Supposingly, the machine chose 'Sie' by putting 'Ihre Nummer' to be "on the safe side" so to say, and to avoid implying too much "proximity" (Yule 1996:9).

Example 3:   Poem, from German to English

INPUT:

Dunkel war's, der Mond schien helle,
Schneebedeckt die grüne Flur,
Als ein Auto blitzesschnelle
Langsam um die Ecke fuhr.   (by: Christian Morgenstern, 1871-1914)

OUTPUT:

It, the moon was dark seemed brightens,
snow-covered the green corridor,
when a car drove lightning-fast
slow around the corner.

This poem by Morgenstern is still very popular in Germany these days and is probably well-known to most of the people from childhood days on. But for Google, it seems to be a tough task: Obvious problems with syntax (first line: 'It, the moon was dark' expressing 'Dunkel war's', while also 'the moon' refers to the second half of the line); with semantics (second line: 'corridor' expressing 'der Flur', which the tool mixed up with 'die Flur' = land area) as well as with lexical storage (the word 'brightens' does not exist as an adjective in the English language, only as a verb; but in this sense it can only appear as an adjective). The usage of 'slow' as an adjective in the fourth line instead of an adverb ('slowly') might be considered as tolerable. The translation of the third line is indeed correct in accordance to the original sense concerning syntax, semantics and lexical storage. But still, the translated verse of the poem does not maintain all of its original sense, not to mention rhyme, rhythm etc. of a poem.

So, concerning 'genre', it has to be taken into consideration that not all kinds of texts still make sense after being put through a language tool. Lyrical texts or even only sentences, as well as discourses are obviously not compatible.

---

[20] *T/V distinction* = "A distinction between forms used for a familiar ('tu') and a non-familiar ('vous') addressee, in French and in other languages" [like Spanish and German, but not in English; *annotation of the writer*] (Yule 1996:135).

III. 2.)   To Avoid Mistakes

So what is compatible then? In fact there is the possibility of pre-editing the text according to a number of rules, which – if observed – help to make a text compatible for a translation engine/machine. On his own website, webmaster Jon Miles (2003) gives advice on how to keep machine translation mistakes in the computer output at minimum:

- Use short sentences – Limit the sentences to a maximum of twenty-five words, because longer sentences are too complex for the machines, and are more likely to be ambiguous.
- Spell check the document – If a spell checker cannot recognise a word, then a machine translator will leave the word untranslated. Also, the spell checker will often pick up mistakes that do not matter to a human, like leaving out the space between sentences. The spell checker will not correct mistakes like using 'to' when the user means 'too' or 'two', so one will have to find those mistakes for oneself.
- Avoid metaphors and jokes – Metaphors and jokes often do not make sense anymore after translation.
- Keep pronouns to a minimum – Pronouns are used for instance instead of nouns that appeared earlier in a sentence or in a previous sentence, as a shorthand. But different languages use different word orders, so the meaning can be lost. Also some languages use different genders for different objects, unlike English. A machine (translating from English to French) will translate 'it' as 'il'. 'Il' could mean 'he' or 'it' to a French reader, so it may be unclear what the user is referring to.
- Spell things out instead of using abbreviations or initials – Machine translators will not understand abbreviations.
- Keep adjectives and adverbs near the words they refer to – In complex sentences, adjectives can become separated from their nouns and adverbs separated from their verbs.
- Use correct grammar and punctuation – Use simple grammatical structures. Consult a style guide, like Strunk to make sure that one is writing standard clear English. The last sentence said 'make sure that one is writing', not 'make sure one is writing'. The first version is clearer and easier to translate.
- Avoid idioms, slang and jargon – Such words are either impossible to translate, or may be translated wrongly.
- Avoid ambiguous words – We do not notice which words have more than one meaning, because we pick the right meaning for the context. Machine translators do not understand the context, so they may pick the wrong meaning to translate. The word 'right', for instance, can mean 'the opposite of left', or 'correct', or 'privilege', among other meanings. 'Harder' can either mean 'more difficult', or mean 'less soft'. Use a word with a single meaning, such as 'correct', instead of 'right', where possible.
- Avoid compound verbs – These are verbs like 'set off', 'head up', 'give over' and 'bring out'. Compound verbs are usually mistranslated.
- Use the International Standard date format – Dates can cause several problems. Year, month, and day are written in different orders in different countries. Fortunately there is a simple solution to all of these problems: the International Standard date format. It is all numerical, thus not translated. The format is: year, month, day, written as: YYYY-MM-DD (for example 2004-03-09).
- Use a machine translator to translate your text and then translate it back again – This final test will affirm, whether the input text complied with those advices and thus is compatible

with a machine translator and has the ability to be understood by a reader after translation into the source language in compliance with the writer's intentions (see: Miles 2003).

All of these advices result in so-called 'human-aided machine translation' (HAMT):[21] This means that not all the translation work is done by the computer, it is being assisted by a human. What this assistant does is called 'controlled language'; a censored or partly pre-translated version of what is to be the input. Arnold et al. define 'controlled language' as follows:

> "A specially simplified version of a language which is adopted (...) as a partial solution to a perceived communication problem. Both the vocabulary and the syntactic structures may be restricted." (1994:211)

This might also work through interaction with the computer – if the translation software is fairly equipped – for instance, by asking the human assistant to pick the desired meaning of a word from a number of propositions.

IV. Linguistic Aspects in MT

Two major difficulties commanding the effective quality of translations done by MT systems are semantic analysis and ambiguity. According to Arnold et al., there were "many cases [of text passages, which are to translate by the machine] where problems seem to require deeper, more meaning oriented representations, and enrichment of the kind of knowledge systems are equipped with" (1994:129).
The authors divide this in three different kinds:

1. linguistic knowledge, which is independent of context, semantic knowledge;
2. linguistic knowledge, which relates to the context; e. g. of earlier utterances, which is sometimes called pragmatic knowledge; and
3. common sense, general non-linguistic knowledge about the real world. The authors highlight, that the distinction between those three kinds of knowledge is not always clear to make, and also, that this distinction is just an attempt to clarify. They also state that "one should not expect to find much in the way of real world, pragmatic, or even semantic processing in current commercial MT systems".

IV. 1.) Semantics

One approach to representing semantics in MT is to associate words with semantic features, corresponding to their sense components. This method appears in most MT systems, to a greater or lesser extend. Here is an example (taken from Arnold et al. 1994:130), to illustrate:

---

[21] For further information see: V. 1.) of this paper

The words 'man', 'boy' and 'girl' might be represented as

man = {+ human, + masculine, + adult}
boy = {+ human, + masculine, - adult}
girl = {+ human, - masculine, - adult}

According to this pattern, words can be added constraints, which help the machine to define and coordinate the allocation of meaning to subjects or/and objects. For instance: the word 'eat' requires, that its AGENT (the eater) is *animate* and that its PATIENT (that which is eaten) is *edible*. Another aspect of constraints might be: *concrete* (as opposed to *abstract*, like in the words 'beauty' or 'freedom') and *solid* (as opposed to *liquid*, like coffee, etc.).

These constraints can be encoded in the grammar by associating features with appropriate nouns in the dictionary. The entry 'eat' might be described as: eat = *verb*, AGENT = *human*, PATIENT = *edible*. Now the grammar will only accept objects of 'eat' which have the feature *edible*. "These selectional restrictions act as a filter on [the] (...) grammar to rule out unwanted analysis" (see: 130).

As to every other rule, exceptions to selectional restrictions abound; e. g. in metaphorical speech. So, according to the authors, selectional restrictions should rather be used to state preferences between alternative interpretations, than to eliminate interpretations.

Especially translating prepositions correctly is difficult to match in MT, since different natural languages tend to a different style of preposition usage.

To consider one example: The preposition 'at', as it is in 'at midday' as well as in 'at school' (*example taken from* Arnold et al. 1994:131), might be assigned an appropriate semantic relation (also called 'semantic role', 'deep case' or 'thematic role'[22] or SR) during analysis: To indicate that 'at' expresses a temporal relation ('at midday') it can be assigned the feature SR=Time. To express a location relation, the feature SR=Place might be assigned. Arnold et al. (131) display the following translation rules concerning this example in the case of translating it into Spanish ('at' in accordance with 'a' indicating temporal relations, and 'en' indicating location relations):

at, SR=Time ⟺ a
at, SR=Place ⟺ en.

These assignments are based on the type of noun that follows the preposition, which means that, in this case, 'midday' has to be marked in the dictionary with some temporal feature, for example: semtype=time. The noun school, to stick with this case, had to be marked with a locational feature, semtype=location, for instance (see: 131).

Arnold et al. state that the SR expressed by PLACE and TIME were "not always fine grained enough" (132). The relation PLACE, for example, needed to be distinguished in two different cases: '(to be) at school' indicates a position, whereas '(to shoot) at the goal' (*examples taken from* Arnold et al. 1994:132) indicated a movement towards a particular place. So it might be useful to decompose the SR into: PLACE_POSITION for the first case and PLACE_PATH for the second case. These new semantic features would also cover the definition of the type of verb, not only the type of noun, which follows the preposition.

---

[22] *semantic role* = According to Arnold et. al. (1994:215): a description of the relationship that a constituent plays with respect to the verb in the sentence. The subject of an active sentence is often the agent or experiencer. Other roles include instrumental, benefactive, patient: *Peter* (experiencer) *died. The cat* (agent) *chased the dog* (patient).

IV. 2.)   Pragmatics

Pragmatics is also difficult to integrate in the system of translation machines. As Levinson puts it, "pragmatics is the study of the relations between language and context that are basic to an account of language understanding" (2003:21). Here, the term language understanding is used to draw attention to the fact that understanding an utterance involves a great deal more that knowing the meanings of the words uttered and the grammatical relations between them. Furthermore, Arnold et al. state that a sentence had to be interpreted relative to the previous discourse and to the situation in which it is uttered.

The authors illustrate this with the following example (139):

The front cover should be closed.

The translation of this sentence will be affected by whether the hearer/reader will interpret the sentence as a command, as in 'close the front cover', or as a statement, which describes the state the cover is likely to be in.

They add that, also, the meaning of a message seems to be shaped by its producer's intentions and beliefs (139). This brings us forth onto the edge of a major boundary in CS rather unlikely to overcome up to the present day or in the near future: How can a machine be capable of knowing about the producer's intentions and beliefs? How can a machine consider cultural, ethic and moral values which would be essential as a basis to judge from? Several different sources tend to see this boundary as unlikely to overcome, since it marks not only one of the major difficulties in MT, but also in other grand fields of AI – the development of robots for example. From the first days of building or manufacturing artificial persons or animals, so-called automats, about 4,000 years ago (see: Recht 2006:13), one of the major aims was to make those creatures as lifelike as possible, which meant that they were supposed to resemble their role-models. Nowadays, scientists from the fields of ALife[23] and Artificial Intelligence have certainly come remarkably far with building "lifelike artificial creatures", as Brooks puts it (2002:46). But be it robots, computers or translation machines – what they all lack is what we refer to as common sense – know-ledge of the real world. This will be dealt with in detail in the following subchapter.

IV. 3.)   Real World Knowledge

Not all the knowledge required to extract the meaning from texts can be got from the texts or their contexts. Considered a sentence like:

I saw the soldiers aim at the women, and I saw several of | *them* | *fall.*

(Example taken from Arnold et al. 1994:139)

---

[23] *ALife* = Artificial Life, which "has three main goals: studying biological issues, abstracting principles of intelligent behavior and develop practical applications based on these findings. In doing so AL uses computational techniques to understand biological issues and biological techniques to solve computational problems." (Pfeifer et al. 2000: without paging)

In order to translate this sentence into German one has to consider what the pronoun 'them' refers to. The question is: Who fell over – soldiers or women? In general, one would reason, that 'aiming at' is usually followed by 'shooting at', which is usually followed by those aimed (and shot) at falling over; although this conclusion has not primarily to do with the semantic meaning of 'aiming'. So it takes knowledge from the real world to decide on who or what the pronoun, the antecedent ('them' in this case), refers to. To represent and manipulate such knowledge automatically "is one of the outstanding research questions of our time" (Arnold et al. 1994:140).

But unlike most knowledge of syntax and/or semantics, this real world knowledge is generally "defeasible" – "that is, subject to revision" (140). The authors add, that some might argue, real world knowledge was not necessarily linguistic knowledge at all and that it was generally hard to distinguish from linguistic.

Another point was the "huge amount of such knowledge we seem to have" (141). At least some methods of representation, such as semantic nets, work for some kinds of knowledge. A semantic net is a network, consisting of terms like 'bird', 'sparrow' or 'wings', and links to one another standing for relations as they make sense, according to real world knowledge. A relation might work as a 'is a'; for example 'a sparrow is a bird' or might also work as 'part of', like in the following example:

Put the toner in the cartridge in the reservoir.
(Example taken from Arnold et al. 1994:141)

When knowing that the reservoir does not have a cartridge as a part, one could work out that one is supposed to put the toner which is in the cartridge in the reservoir, rather than to put the toner in a particular cartridge, possibly the one that is in the reservoir (see: 141).

The authors conclude, that the major problem with representing real world knowledge automatically was, that it was only a "loosely organised collection of knowledge" and that it was "not how at least some kinds of human knowledge seem to be" (142).

V.   Computational Linguistics

The complex field of CL can only be viewed briefly due to the size limitation of this paper. At least I would like to provide an approach to two general computational aspects of MT: the usual methods established MT systems work with, as well as a closer look upon working procedures of three of today's commonly most acknowledged translation systems:

V. 1.)   Methods of MT

What all MT systems have in common is the usage of bilingual dictionaries (in the form of files) and modules to maintain basic grammatical rules, but their methods remarkably differ:

- **Direct MT** – word-for-word translation from the dictionary in order of their input; subsequently syntax and flexion are being adjusted to stored rules of the target language. This method makes up the most old and simple way of MT.
- **Transfer** – the most classical method of MT, which operates within three steps: analysis (of the grammatical structure of the source text, mostly done within a tree-model), transfer (two separated processes, in which firstly words and secondly grammatical rules are be-

ing transferred into the target language), generation (those rules are being applied to the words in the target language and the result finally makes up the target text);

- **Interlingua** – a neutral intermediary language, to which the source text is translated for the time being, and from which the grammatical information of the target language is generated. This method is considered as helpful in case of complex utterances.

- **EBMT** (example-based machine translation) – consisting mainly of a translation memory, which stores often recurring sentences and similes along with their meanings in the target language and calculates statistically (information retrieval method) in what extent the entries in the translation memory are similar to each of the sentences of the source text. The translation is being generated on the basis of the nearest matchings. According to Trujillo this view of translation was "a reasonable approximation to the saying that 'a good translator is a lazy translator'" – which meant that "the production of a new translation should employ as much material from previous translations as possible" (Trujillo 1999:203).

- **SBMT** (statistic-based machine translation) – an additional program analyses a diversified Corpus,[24] as big as possible, of bilingual texts, like the Bible. Words and grammatical forms are being assigned to each other on the basis of their frequency of occurrence and proximity within the text, which establishes a dictionary and rules concerning grammatical transfer, on whose basis texts are being translated. SBMT does not require any knowledge of the concerned languages, thus became popular recently, but the quality of the output is correspondingly deficient. The Pentagon tends to use systems based on that method, when there is not enough time to have grammatical rules etc. collected by humans.

- **HAMT** (human-aided machine translation) is yet another method of MT. Amongst other aspects, this will be dealt with in the following chapter of this paper.

V. 2.)   Commonly Acknowledged Translation Systems

This section considers current well-known production systems on the world market. Some of them originate from the "failures" (Slocum 1988:14), that were other attempts to develope forward-looking systems, like 'TAUM'[25] or GAT (= 'Georgetown Automatic Translation'). Others are the result of successful and continuing MT R&D projects.

A "standard installation" (15) includes provision for pre-processing, translation with human intervention, and post-editing. "To MT users, acceptability is a function of the amount of pre- and/or post-editing that must be done (which is also the greatest determinant of cost)". On the other hand the author states that a human translator seems to improve his own skills while he compensates for the incapacity of the MT system, for instance: recognising MT errors and devising more efficient ways of correcting them.

Furthermore, Slocum argues that "some users, indeed, are repeat customers" and "MT systems cannot be argued not to work, for they are in fact being bought and used, and they save time and/or money for their users".

Three of these commonly acknowledged MT systems are displayed here:

---

[24] *Corpus* = here: a limited or complete collection of oral and/or written utterances, used for linguistic analysis
[25] *TAUM* = Traduction Automatique de l'Université de Montreal, which was a precursor to METEO

V. 2. a)   LOGOS

The translation system LOGOS was first installed in 1971 by the U. S. Air Force, after a development phase of about seven years, in order to translate English maintenance manuals for military equipment into Vietnamese during the Vietnam War, but ended two years later "due to the termination of U. S. involvement in that war" (Slocum 1988:18). According to Slocum, the linguistic foundations of LOGOS were "not well advertised, presumably for reasons involving trade secrecy" (1988:18). But LOGOS kept on attracting customers and in the year 1978, the Siemens AG from Germany took on the funding of the development of a German-English system on the basis of LOGOS for the use of telecommunication manuals.

According to Slocum, the first result after three years of development was considered not suitable for use due to the "poor quality of translations" (1988:18). As opposed to this, Schwanke states that the results of the LOGOS project during the 'Siemens AG' sponsored development phase were being presented at the Hanover fair (Germany) in 1982 (see: 1991:97), without mentioning that the 'Siemens AG' refrained from sponsoring in 1981. Slocum (1988:18): "(...) not suitable for use due to (...) the economic situation within Siemens AG which had resulted in a much-reduced demand for translation, hence no immediate need for an MT system".

The 'Wang' computer company forged an agreement with LOGOS then, in order to allow the implementation of the German-English system to be used on 'Wang' office computers. This final system reached the commercial market, and has been purchased by several multi-national organizations, e. g. Nixdorf, Triumpf-Adler or Hewlett-Packard (see: Slocum 1988:18).

According to Schwanke, LOGOS operates within the following language pairs: German-English, German-French, German-Italian, English-German, English-French, English-Spanish (see: 1991:97). It runs on IBM mainframe computers, subordinated to the system software MVS and VM/CMS and Unix V.2; on Wang computers to the Wang-VS system software. The author cites that it was considered useful particularly for the translation of spezialized texts, like manuals.

The author classifies the translation process of the system LOGOS into eight different steps (see: 98):

1. Conversion of the text into a form, which is readable for the machine; e. g. marking of small and capital letters;
2. Access to the different dictionaries;
3. Classification of the parts of speech by sequential word analysis considering the syntactic context;
4. Identification of the nominal phrases;
5. Reducing the sentence down to a simplified sentence structure, provided the analysis of relative clauses;
6. Analysis and reducing of prepositional phrases and subordinate clauses and semantic-syntactic verb analysis;
7. Sequencing of the different blocks according to the syntactic rules of the target language;
8. Output.

Schwanke adds that it was not possible to characterise the linguistic aspects of the system due to the utmost secrecy of these details and information; not even the involved German co-operators were initiated. Thus it was not possible to add extensive new entries, because one would require access to the linguistic basis of the system and justify the algorithms[26]. Such enquiries had to be sent to the American headquarters of the company (see: 99).

---

[26] *algorithm* = according to Arnold et al. (1994:209): a prescribed set of well-defined rules or instructions for the solution of a problem

V. 2. b)   METAL

The METAL project at the Linguistics Research Center of the University of Texas is one of the "major MT R&D[27] groups around the world" (Slocum 1988:28), which lead to a commercial-grade system: the METAL German-English system. Having passed tests in a "production-style setting" (Slocum 1988:28), it was installed at the sponsor's site in Germany in order of further testing and the developing of a translator interface. Then, in April 1985 it was introduced for sale as LITRAS at the Hanover fair in Germany.

One of the advantages of METAL is "its accommodation of a variety of linguistic/strategies" (Slocum 1988:28): On the one hand: The German analysis component is based on a "context-free phrase-structure grammar, augmented (...) for (...) arbitrary transformations" (28). On the other hand: The English analysis component employs a modified Generalized Phrase-Structure Grammar (GPSG)[28] approach. Transfer[29] is separated from analysis and the system is multi-lingual; thus a "given constituent structure analysis can be used for transfer and synthesis" (29) into several target languages.

In 1985, the Siemens AG in Germany established a new METAL project at the Catholic University of Louvain (Belgium) for the developing of a Dutch-French/ French-Dutch system, while until that day, METAL 'only' worked within the language pairs German-Chinese/German-Spanish/English-German.

METAL's transfer component includes two transformation packages: One of them is used by transfer grammar rules, the other one is used by transfer dictionary entries. These two packages co-operate during the transfer due to a top-down exploration of the highest-scoring tree, which is produced during the analysis phase. This requires the assistance of the linguist, who controls the strategy for the top-down pass and writes the transfer rules, which are often "paired 1-1 with the grammar rules used to perform the original analysis" (29). The advantage here is the fact, that there is no searching through a general transfer grammar to find applicable rules required, which avoids applicating the wrong ones.

However, to operate on the translation of clauses, the option of employing a more general transfer grammar is available.

To provide that every input results in some translation, despite the case that no analysis is achieved for a given input, the longest phrases, which together span that input, are selected for independent transfer and synthesis.

In addition, the Texas research group has developed software packages to make METAL a complete system, "rather than a basic machine translation engine, that leaves much drudgery for its human developers/users" (30).

V. 2. c)   METEO

METEO is one of the few systems, which has only one customer: the 'Canadian Meteorological Center' ('CMC'), a nation-wide weather communications network. According to Arnold et al. (1994:11), METEO is a MT system, which had been in daily use since 1977, translating up to 45,000 words daily. As a spin-off of the TAUM technology, which was "probably the first MT project designed strictly around the transfer[30] approach" (12), the system is in actual fact named TAUM-METEO. It is the world's only example of a truly fully-automatic MT system.

---

[27] *R&D* = research and development
[28] *GPSG* = generative grammatical theory, which sets deep structure and transformations aside, and represents a formalised model for specification of the surface entities (see: López 2008).
[29] also see: V. 1.) of this paper
[30] also see chapter V. 1.) of this paper

METEO scans the network traffic for English weather reports, translates them directly into French, and sends the translation back out over the communications network automatically. ME-TEO detects its own errors and passes the offending input to human editors, although this means that METEO does not attempt corrections. Output, which METEO deems 'correct', is dispatched without any human intervention (see: Slocum 1988:19).

But there appears to be one major disadvantage: "METEO is not extensible – though similar systems could be built for equally restricted textual domains, if they exist". According to Slocum, the built-in limitations of METEO's theoretical basis had been reached by the year 1981 and further improvement was "not likely to be cost-effective".

VI.   Epilogue: On the Future of MT

Particularly during the 1980s, when further great steps in the development of MT were made, human translators started to fear for their jobs which might be taken over by translating machines leaving their human role-models obsolete. So far, this paper has shown major leaps in the research field of MT, yet its restrictions and limitations just as plainly, too, leaving bleak future predictions on improvement. According to Arnold et al. (1994:8), the answer to the question whether translation machines might take over one day would be a definite 'no': One reason is the currently possible quality of MT. Another reason is the growing volume of required translation, and the limitations of current and foreseeable MT systems. But the authors also argue, that MT could in fact "enslave human translators by controlling the translation process, and forcing them to work on the problems it throws up, at its speed", although the authors object that it was not likely to happen with MT.

They also state that it was quite common that texts which are submitted for translation need to be adapted; for instance in terms of format or typographically, before the MT system can deal with them. After the translation process the output was "invariably deemed to be grammatically and translationally imperfect" (12). Since MT systems would "never be able to handle all types of text reliably and accurately", their output required post-editing, which was done best by a human translator.

What is, according to the authors, rather likely to happen is that the translating processes of everyday work, like translating weather reports for instance, would become automated and often tedious, leaving human translators free to spend more time on increasing clarity and improving style, and to translate more important and interesting documents, like editorials. The authors confirm with an example taken from the Canadian Meteorological Centerimproved, when METEO was installed: The human translators would spend more and more time on finding ways to improve the system output, rather than translating the weather bulletins by hand (9).

The authors conclude with the statement that "MT is possible and potentially useful, despite current limitations" (16). They subjoin that there were "many open research problems in MT, but "the general public should stop over-expecting" (1). Also, they admit that building an MT system was obviously not an easy enterprise, involving the constructing of grammars and dictionaries, to which there could not exist a "magic solution" (11). Slocum confirms the improbability of 'perfect translation' as a reachable goal – for humans, as well as for machines:

> "Human languages are, by nature, different. So much so, that the illusory goal of abstract perfection in translation – once and still imagined by some to be achievable – can be comfortably ruled out of the realm of possible existence." (1988:35)

Personally, do not see future jobs of human translators being threatened by translation machines or computers whatsoever. To confirm this I would like to quote Wilss' words on the issue of computers and consciousness:

> "The fear of computers making themselves independent within self-created artificial worlds and competing with humans is improbable. A computer cannot program itself, it is and remains a labourer, dependent of the programming capacities of humans. It cannot think or ratiocinate over itself. Just as one cannot make the experience of 'colours' comprehensible to a blind man, one cannot make the experience of consciousness accessible to a computer." (1988:235).

Furthermore, within the past twenty years, the population of the First World has grown so close to machines, in fact it is striking how much we have become dependent of our PCs, mobile phones, the internet, medicine, genetic engineering etc.; a state of being somewhere in between human and machine which Donna Haraway metaphorically referred to as the cyborg[31] status (see: 1991:150).
Brooks confirms by saying that

> "with all these trends we will become a merger between flesh and machines. We will have the best that machineness has to offer, but we will also have our bioheritage to augment whatever level of machine technology we have so far developed. So we (the robot-people) [or cyborgs] will be a step ahead of them (the pure robots). We won't have to worry about them taking over." (2002:x).

Personally, I do not suppose that MT will ever happen to reach a status of 'non-human-aided' translation ability. The TV series *Star Trek* and its spin-offs offers an optimistic view on humankind's future; one of those aspects is the vision of all nations of our planet Earth joined in one, and even teaming up with other planets' joined nations to strive together for peaceful existence and freedom – which is not at least made possible through a 'to-good-to-be-true' translating system (the 'communicator'), that translates natural languages up to a certain level of complexity right away in the moment of utterance, so that finally all participants of the conversation in fact hear the speaker(s) talk in their native language. But this is TV fiction and hardly to become reality, at least in the near future.

---

[31] *cyborg* = a blend of the terms *cybernetic* and *organism*; it refers to a creature consisting of biological and technological components.

VII. Bibliography

VII. 1.) Literature

Arnold, D. et al.
(1994): *Machine Translation. An Introductory Guide*. Manchester, UK: NCC Blackwell.

Brooks, Rodney
(2002): *Flesh and Machines. How Robots will Change us*. New York, US: Vintage.

Haraway, Donna
(1991): „A Cyborg Manifesto: Science, Technology, and Socialist-Feminism in the Late Twentieth Century". In: Haraway, Donna: *Simians, Cyborgs, and Women. The Reinvention of Nature*. London, UK: Free Association Books.

Hutchins, William John (ed.)
(2000): *Early Years in Machine Translation. Memoirs and Biographies of Pioneers*. Amsterdam, Netherlands, Philadelphia, US: Benjamins.

Levinson, Stephen C.
(2003): *Pragmatics*. Cambridge, UK: CUP.

Luckhardt, Heinz-Dirk & Zimmermann, Harald H.
(1991): *Computergestützte und maschinelle Übersetzung. Praktische Anwendung und angewandte Forschung*. [Sprachwissenschaft-Computerlinguistik, Vol. 14]. Saarbruecken: AQ.

Patterson, B.
(1982): "Multilingualism in the European Community". *Multilingua. Journal of Cross Cultural and Interlanguage Communication*. 1(1):1982. [4-15]. Berlin, New York, US: Mouton de Gruyter.

Recht, Marcus
(2006): *Homo Artificialis. Eine Androiden & Cyborg Analyse mit dem Fokus auf Star Trek*. Saarbruecken: VDM Verlag Dr. Müller.

Schwanke, Martina
(1991): *Maschinelle Übersetzung. Ein Überblick über Theorie und Praxis*. Berlin, Heidelberg: Springer.

Slocum, Jonathan (ed.)
(1988): *Machine Translation Systems. Studies in Natural Language Processing*. Cambridge, UK, New York, US: CUP.

Trujillo, Arturo
(1999): *Translation Engines: Techniques for Machine Translation*. [Applied Computing]. London, UK: Springer.

Wilss, Wolfram
(1988): *Kognition und Übersetzen. Zu Theorie und Praxis der maschinellen Übersetzung*. Tuebingen: Max Niemeyer.

Yule, George
(1996): *Pragmatics*. Oxford, UK, New York, US: OUP.

VII. 2.)   Internet Sources

Gibbon, Davydd: "Warren Weaver's three Levels of Problems in Communication".
[No Information on Year of Publication Given].
Access on: November 11th 2007.
<http://coral.lili.uni-bielefeld.de/Classes/Summer98/Functions/ functions/node7 .html>.

Keep, Christopher et al.
(2001): "The Electronic Labyrinth".
Access on January 11th 2008.
<http://www.iath.virginia.edu/elab/hfl0034.html>.

López, Justo Fernández
(2008): Lexikon der Linguistik und Nachbardisziplinen.
Access on October 3rd 2008.
<http://culturitalia.uibk.ac.at/hispanoteca/lexikon%20der%20linguistik/Eingangsseite/Lexikon-Linguistik-Eingangsseite.htm>.

Lewis, Judy
(2004): The RAND Corporation.
Access on January 11th 2008.
<http://www.rand.org/about/index.html>.

Miles, Jon
(2003): "Write for Machine Translation".
Access on Novomber 25th 2007.
<http://home.clara.net/jmiles/guide.htm>.

Nirenburg, Sergei
(2003): "Bar Hillel and Machine Translation: Then and Now".
Institute for Language (ILIT), University of Maryland Baltimore County (UMBC).
Access on January 25th 2008.
<http://ilit.umbc.edu/SergeiPub/bar-hillel.pdf>.

Pfeifer, Rolf et al.
(2000): "Artificial Life".
Access on: October 3rd 2008. [Without Paging].
<http://www.ifi.uzh.ch/groups/ailab/teaching/AL00.html>.

Savetz, Kevin: Digital Deli.
[No Information on Year of Publication Given].
Access on January 7th 2008.
<http://www.digitaldeli.co.uk>.

<http://webcenters.netscape.compuserve.com>.

<www-history.mcs.st-and.ac.uk>.

<http://www.cray.com>.

<http://www.eamt.org>.

<http://www.google.de>.

<http://www.pcai.com>.